WORDS FROM UP ABOVE

YOU IN MY LIFE

Letting you in my life
was the smartest step
I made.

On me your hands
were laid.

You taught me on
who I must depend.

You are my true
friend.

On me your light
shine;

When I let you have my time.

You came and grabbed me out of the jaws of despair.

With your wonderful care.

My life has been turned around.

And there's no reason for me to frown.

You gave me restoration.

Along with your precious salvation.

There is so much I have been empowered to do.

But it's only through you.

I give you all praise, honor, and glory.

So, now I can tell man
the whole story.

OVER THE HILLS

If we could see the things that are over the hills in our lives before, we approach it; would we still go on? Or would we stop and give up? Would we make a quick detour to try to avoid the situations that wait for us? Or would we tried to find the solution to the problems before we encounter them? Some of us may still go and even though we may see the problems or mishaps that go along with them. In looking at how far we have come, would we still have gone through with these things? Some things would probably would not try to change when we are going through them if we could see the outcome. If we could see the outcome in advance would be still go through them? Would we ask ourselves more questions about our situation? Would we stand up and face the test knowing that it's only for a little while? Knowing that it won't last forever, that things would change and work out for the best, would we still stand? We could look at the hills and see them as more strength, and not as an impossible problem. If we see it as strength maybe we could strive to do our best. In knowing that it will make us stronger we could face our problems or situations much better. If we could see the prize, the game and triumph that's waiting for us on the other side of the hill we…………………well, most of us would be willing to take the challenge. Don't see the hill. Don't concentrate on it.

See the victory and triumph!!!! Climb over the hills, so that you can stand on top of the mountain.

GRATEFUL

If we all took a little time to step back and see all the goals and achievements, we made we would be more grateful? So many times, and I should say too many times, we focus on things of little or no importance. A beggar does not focus on what he does not have, instead he focusses on how to get it. He is always thankful for every little bit. He knows that somehow; he will make it through each day. He has a that God will make a way. He will send someone his way to lend a hand. We can learn a lot from him in our daily walk. We must praise the Creator of all for everything that we have. Also, continue to thank and praise him for even the smallest achievement. I believe that the majority of this population has some kind of achievement. It may be a kind word you spoke to someone, giving your seat up to someone who really needs to sit down on the bus, a word of wisdom you spoke to someone; or the saver you encountered via your boss through God may be one of your achievements. Every achievement you make you never make it alone. If it had not been for God, you would not be an achiever. There will not be anything for you to look back at and be very proud of. As we look back, let's look back and see how God has caused us to achieve. It is then we would know the true meaning of being *grateful*.

NO LIMIT

As you look at things in this earth you can see that they all have limits. Once the limit has expired on one thing and another begins. It is a continuous process. Daytime stops and nighttime begins. And then here comes daybreak with the beginning of yet another day. The trees blossom and bring forth fruit. Another season comes in and the leaves began to fall off the trees. Still, there's another that covers them with snow. Yet another makes them grow.

The flowers blossom with the growing of grass. There is a season that takes over and they both died and wither away. Another season around the corner has its turn to make them grow again. The sun rises every morning and in the evening there's a time that the sun must set. There's a time to go to work. And there is a time to leave work. Everything seems to be limited on this earth. Let's look at the sky. It is always there. It's everywhere.

Everyone can see it all at the same time. It has no limit. We can see God through the eyes of the sky. He has no limit. We can ask anything of Him. He will do it because He has no limit. He never dies or leaves us after a certain season has expired. He is the only one had, has and never will have any limit. His love even goes on for us. It never dies. He is the God has **no limit.**

TAKING TIME TO CREATE

When I created you, I gave you special attention and time. You were not like any of my other creations. You were so special yet wonderfully made. The beauty I saw when I created you prompted me to breathe the breath of life into you. My other creations were wonderful. But the beauty of you was like no other. I decided to choose you (the most awesome of my creations) to live inside of and to be one with. I also gave you the privilege of choice; the opportunity to choose. I gave you an inner man. I did this so that you could see, think, and feel as I do. I gave you an agape love, which is my love. It is a love that you can feel deep inside and allow to grow. It is also a love that will allow me to work through you to be extended to others from the inside out. You can see somewhat why I gave you the name man:

Master of my earth which I created is who you are.

Awesome mind and thinking is what I birthed inside of you.

Never give in to any negativity or evilness that you may encounter.

That is why gave you the name **man**. You are my most awesome creation. So, whatever you may

face in this life know
that you are my **man**
and why I created
you. It is then you will
come for all.

TAKING TIME TO CREATE

What I created you I knew that you will be the tunnel for me to come through. I gave you unlimited strength and balance. The reason I chose you instead of man to carry the scene is because of your feminist and sensitivity. You are very delicate and you understand that a child needs to be handled delicate through child birth. I created you to help give my man balance. You know how to encourage and reach beyond. You have been the way for me to win back my people. You must always lift your head up and never let anything or anyone discourage you because you are **Woman**:

Wisdom you give to many.

Only lean and depend on me for direction.

I'll never leave your side. I'll always be a prayer away.

Miracle bearer you sometimes become.

Answers you give to so many because I birthed them inside of you.

Never giving up or in is one of your precious qualities.

THOUGHTS

If you knew the exact day at times with the cart this life, what things would you change?

To love is to.................................

....

.....

Be planted as a seed and blossom and grow into a tree.

The path you choose today will leave you on your journey of tomorrow.

Confession is a seed and we determine the harvest.

To smile is to love.

To frowned his disappointments.

EACH DAY

When I woke up this morning, I first gave praise to the Father. Then I thought of all the things I will have to do today. Every one of them required His help. 'Father help me to do all that I must do this day,' is my prayer. He replied, 'yes. I will my child. You are my responsibility. I've been waiting on you to ask me this. It gives me so much joy in knowing that you asked me (your Father) and not someone else. Now, I must reward you for your obedience to me and to my word.'

After hearing all this I knew that today would be a blessed day; at work, at home, or wherever I may go. Nothing would stop me now. If I ran into any problems today, I knew that I could ask my Father to help me and He would. I have a piece inside that is worth more than all the money in the world. Now I have an assurance and confidence that I'm not a long period today is the beginning of the rest of my life. Each day I will pray this way so that I will succeed.

ONE TOUCH

To have just one touch from you is what my innermost being yearns and cries out for. I know that the feeling that I would get from your touch could never be explained in any of the words that man has ever known. The touch from you couldn't even compare to the love that one person has for another. To know that I'm being touched by you gives me complete rest and assurance. With one touch from you there will be nothing I couldn't get through. I can't even compare your touch with that of my mother. Your touch is incomparable yet so unique and unexplainable. The times that I may have felt low, just for a moment you touch me just wants. In an instant I knew everything would be all right. In your touch lies so many things; healing, peace, comfort, love, joy, meekness, confidence and so much more. All it takes is one touch to get all of these things from you. When you give me a touch it reaches every part of my inner and outer being. I ask that you never take away your touch. I ask and pray that you give me at least one touch a day. It is then I will have more of an assurance to make it through the day. There are so many things that are revealed to me through your touch.

Every time you touch me change my life more and more. It increases my faith in you. It causes hope to grow and spring forth in my heart. I have been ultimately changed by your touch. Father, continue to give me **ONE TOUCH.**

THE MOST PRECIOUS MOMENTS

The dawn of a new day and the still of the night are two of the most precious moments to view your glory. Everything is quiet and still at these two particular times. No one seems to be in a 'hurry mode.' The rising of the sun shows how peaceful it is to have YOU in one's life. You are so awesome and mighty yet so gentle and full of care. At night we can look up and see the stars and the moon. We can see the way you placed them in the sky. If we listen close enough, we can hear the echo of all the things you created. The still of the night and the dawn of a new day may be the best way to view your glory because there are any interruptions. Not one single distraction is there. It is more powerful to view it alone than with another. Viewing it alone can have a greater impact and revelation. Sitting at the window and viewing the still of the night can say so much to a person. You can begin to see many mysteries unfolding. Why God created night and day? You may see the reason as; to give man time to sit back and think of Him. Or it may be so that man and He could have dialogue. Or it may be to give man time to view His glory on interrupted by anything. One last reason may be to see the awesome creations that God placed in the sky. Whatever mystery may unfold for you as you view these two precious moments will change your life, but only if you allow it to.

CAN YOU STAND TO TRUST GOD

Look at the birds and how they trust and rely on Him. They opened their eyes each day knowing that there will be food for them. They never sleep in fear. They never worry how it will come or whose hands it will come by; for to them it comes by His hands. They always know each day they will have enough. So, they never take some and save it or stored it up for later. 'Hard times' is not part of their vocabulary. They don't even know what that means. They always sing praises to Him, right from their heart. Praising Him is a ritual; a practice and even a way of life for them. It's somewhat like some humans think they have to have their morning cup coffee. Well, the birds have to give God His praises or they will be like those humans who have to have their morning coffee. They won't be able to function. It all the way that the birds praise Him it's nothing compared to how He longs to hear His number one creation praise Him. You are worth so much more to Him than anything He created. He has given you His Spirit. You were created with inner and outer beauty. He will always take care of you. Nothing that you go through has to be faced alone. He takes care of the birds. He will take far greater care of you than He does the birds; for you are so valuable and precious to Him. Cry out to Him and tell Him how you feel. Tell Him the hurts and the pain and then He will lead you to His Word that will be your guide for your situation. Trust Him to be everything to you. He longs for you to trust Him with your very life and all you have. I ask you this one question: **CAN YOU STAND TO TRUST GOD?**

A CONVERSATION
WITH GOD

I had a conversation with God and He begins to say:

How can I work in you when you won't submit to me? How can I use you greatly when you won't speak what I said to? How can I be a voice in the earth when you won't allow me to flow through you? I have spoken my word. I have birthed it inside of you. My only desire is for you to allow it to flow through you into my earth which I created. I want to use you to prepare this world for my return. The only thing I require of you is that you will submit, speak and let my words flow through you.

I begin to say:

Oh, my God how can I do what you have asked of me? Maybe......God, I think you have the wrong person. I'm not ready for this. Choose someone else that is more prepared.

He said:

Oh, my child I call the things that are not as though they were. I am. I will do the work. I will talk the talk. You just walk the walk. I don't call the things that your natural mind can see but I call out the things that are in your spirit. When you begin to speak my words, you will see me begin to work and flow through you. I AM has created you. Will you be a willing vessel unto me?

I said:

Yes!!! Father I will allow you to flow through me. I will submit and speak the word. For it is You who does the work through me. Now I see myself as you do. Now I will begin to call the things that are not as though they were. Now I see miracles happening because I spoke only your words to the situation. I was not moved by circumstances. Now I've learned the true meaning of trusting in you.

Then He ended the conversation:

You are in Canaan now my child. You are glorifying me. You are giving great pleasure to my name. Men and women are seeing who I am to you and who I will be to them if they will allow me to.

EVERYTHING SLEEPS AND AWAKES

Everything God made
sleeps and awakes.
When I look at the
trees, I can see how
they sleep. In the fall
when there are
leaves falling from
the trees it is then
they began to sleep.
They are sound
asleep in winter.
Spring burst in with

the tossing and
turning from the
trees as they awake
from their sleep. They
are so full of life now.
Now they are so
longer sleeping. The
trees can even snore
sometimes. As you
hear the rustling and
shaking of the trees
you can know that

they are snoring.
When the flowers are
planted in the earth it
is then they sleep. As
they are watered,
they begin to toss in
the dirt and soil,
which is their bed. As
they begin to blossom
one bud at a time
they begin to awake
and get out of bed.

Once they are at their full blossom they are standing up and fully awake. Everything God made sleeps and awakes. When the wind does not howl and you can't feel a breeze it is then the wind sleeps. Sometimes it wakes up quietly and softly with a gentle breeze. At other times it awakes in a hurry so strong and fierce, now it is fully awake. The sky sleeps at night. If you look up you can see it sleeping so peacefully. You can see the beauty and stillness of it at night.

As the morning approaches you can see the sky slowly opening its eyes. When it fully conquerors the night fall and not a glimpse of darkness is left in the sky it is then the sky is awake. The sun even sleeps. At night as it leaves our sight when it sets it is then it sleeps as the sun rises and bursts through the clouds it awakes. The number one and most important creation of all who sleeps and awakes is man. There is so much beauty in watching man as he sleeps and awakes.

Just remember that everything God made sleeps and awakes in some form and in some way in its own set time.

I'M BLESSED

When I look around and see the many things that are happening it makes me grateful. As I looked on so many situations, I can truly say that I'm blessed. Even though dangerous all around me and the evilness and hatred may be in the very air that I breathe, it can't harm me. I feel protected because all of my trust is in the One that made us all. I am blessed. Some can't or won't try to perceive the point that I am stressing. The only way to truly be blessed is to depend on Him. I am blessed. It's not just because I have my five senses operating properly. But it is also because of who God is in my life. I am truly blessed. So, as you look around and see so many things that may be a part of your life, just look up and depend on Him and then you will be able to say from the heart the word:

I AM TRULY BLESSED!!!!!!!!!!!!!!!!!! !!!!!!!!!!!!!!!!!!!

WHICH WILL YOU LISTEN TO?

When they both cried
out with desires
which will you
choose?

When they both
yearn for your
attention which will
you please?

Which will you pick over the other?

Will it be the inner or the outer man?

Which will win the battle in which will win the war?

Which will have a stronger impact?

Which one holds your ultimate strength?

Ask yourself these and many more questions if you want to win. Ask the question, 'which one?' See, you can only pick one. Which one will you choose? You can't satisfy both of them. This one was the other. The decision lies inside of you.

Which would you choose to give pleasure at all your attention to?

Will it be outer or inner?

You will decide! Make no mistake about!! You will decide and it will be known to others the one you chose by the way you live.

VIOLENCE

When will it all end and when will it all cease? Will it always be with us? We try to shelter ourselves and our children each day from the violence. Can we successfully do this 100%? No!!!!! There is violence all around us. Our child(ren) will see the violence when they go to school, outside to play, or going to the store. There is even violence in some cartoons we allow our child(ren) to watch. We may say; 'we will let them watch the cartoons instead of movies with gun, killing, blood and fighting in them.' If we really think about it, it is in some of the cartoons also. Let's teach our child(ren) the meaning of self-control, the word no, and how to express their dislikes or disagreements without resorting to violence. In doing this we can truly try to make somewhat of a difference. If we say that our child(ren)'s lives and perhaps one other child's (that's not ours) from violence, we have made a great accomplishment. So, let's end violence with our child(ren) first. And then help someone else's child. All it takes is ours and one more child to stop the violence. Oh, and let's not forget to pray for our child(ren) each day and each night of their lives.

LIVING LIFE TO THE FULLEST

If you examine your life today, can you honestly say that you have lived life to the fullest? What is your definition of living life to the fullest? What is your definition of living life to the fullest? Could it be how many parties you attend? Could it even be how popular you become with the fellows or the ladies? Could it even be how much money that you have accumulated? My definition of living life to the fullest is to do whatever makes you happy as long as you are pleasing God at the same time. No matter what the people may say or think of you, just do it. My philosophy is, 'don't try so hard to please people, but rather please God.' When you please Him, you can rest assured my friend that you will touch and make a difference in many, many lives. Always live your life to the fullest by pleasing your Awesome Creator; God. Now, that's truly living.

CHALLENGES

So many people have been faced with so many things. They asked themselves many of the questions which they have no answers for. To ask the questions is a good thing. To search out the answers has a far greater reward. If we never ask the questions, our minds would just dwindle and ultimately, we'll lose the spirit of going on. To go is to find out and challenge our minds. Every day will bring about new questions and new challenges. We must be prepared. The only way to truly prepare for the challenges is to have God on your side. Make no mistake about it; you will have challenges as long as you are here on earth. It's far better to face the challenges with the One who can solve every challenge that you face. He can only do it only if you allow Him. We all have the power to allow or to not allow Him. There is a challenge waiting to be accepted by us all. It is the challenge of knowing the power that we possess. God made us in His own image. He is so awesome. We are so awesome. You can and cannot allow. We can and cannot allow. He has authority. We have authority. We are a duplicate of Him. The challenge that He presents to us every day is; 'what are you going to do

with this, which I
want to give and had
given to you? Will you
accept the challenge
or would you just
brush it off?' It's up
to you. Again, I ask;
are you up for the
challenge? Will you
ever be up for?

FINER THINGS

What are truly the finer things in life? I think it is the small things. When we begin to appreciate the small things, we began to understand the meaning of the finer things of life. We tend too many times to focus on all the big things that life brings to us. It's the smaller things that lead to the bigger ones. When we began to appreciate them, it opens all kinds of avenues for us. Are the finer things for you about the house, car, money, business? Or could it be about touching someone's heart? Or could it be about making a difference in someone else's life? There's nothing wrong with having the house, car, money, family, and/or the business. When you have touched or made a difference in someone else's life you have received the finer things of life. It may not mean much to some, but to the recipient of the impact that you made in their life; it can mean the world to them. Search and strive for the true

finer things of this
life.

THANKSGIVING AND BEING BLESSED

There are so many things that we take for granted. We do it sometimes without being aware of it. Our sight, being able to speak, here, and walk are the four major things we take for granted all too often. As we look at others who are without these four valuable things, sometimes we become thankful sometimes we don't. To be able to do all of these things is to be blessed. So as you look around and you may focus on the things you may not have; you will know that if you have these for you are blessed. There's nothing wrong with having other things. But be thankful for whatever you may have. Don't look at what you don't have. When you are thankful and know that you are blessed you open the doors for more blessings. When you can hear your name being called the first time, you are blessed. When you can speak and be understood clearly, you are blessed. So be thankful to the Master, and then you will be able to put your hand in His hand. Use all of these for major things (seeing, speaking, walking, and hearing) to give Him praise. If you do this then you are truly blessed. Because now you understand what it means to be **BLESSED.**

SALVATION

O

T

S

P

E

T

S

The steps that I have taken a life were not always prosperous. I took steps from the time of an infant to a toddler. Those steps were some of the most precious ones for my parents, and they were there to see me take them.

Then there were steps from a toddler to childhood. Those steps are very important, because the steps you take at this stage in life will help to mold you into a promising young adult. Once you pass childhood and you go through a phase of puberty and whatever steps were taken from infant, toddler, and childhood are now being seen. A different person may guide you through these steps. Now is the test, the finishing product; adulthood. But think about it you're not really alone. For God is there making plans and preparations for each one of your steps. After all, He is the one that has been there with you every step of your life, (infant, toddler, childhood, and now adulthood). He has not stopped holding your hand and guiding you along the way. So, my friend, in case you have not yet decided, take a step of faith. And receive Him into your life so you can have a brand-new step. This will be a step that you can really experience in a way you have not yet known. It's the step of salvation. You don't have to wait until you reach a certain age to experience the fullness of it all. Take a step right now, this day. Take the step of salvation.

SEEING IS BELIEVING
BELIEVING IS SEEING

Which do you believe?

If it is believing is seeing then you are person of little faith. Why? Faith is something that you cannot see. With believing is seeing you only believe in what you can see.

You have no vision. Your eyesight is very limited. You will stay in the same rut and ultimately the same place. So, step up and open your mind to being is believing.

If you are more with being is believing you can go beyond this world's limitations. When you believe what you cannot see you are a visionary. You can see and dream beyond your imaginations and bring them into reality by being a firm believer in seeing is believing. When you believe and what you cannot see you drink all kinds of power into your hands. You cause things to happen in a realm that is beyond the what your mind can imagine. It's all spiritual. You can believe your way out of the toughest storm that may come. But it is all in the way you believe and say things. It's the ability to exercise your faith in who are in God.

TRUST ME

Will you trust me with your life? When you allow me to remove all the doubt that you have had for so long? Will you allow me to order your steps? Can you cast all your care upon me? Will you give me the opportunity of being the Father that you yearned for me to be so long? I can do all of these things if you just trust Me. I can take you places you never dreamed you could go. I will give you your heart's desire. When the road seems a little too rough you can pass it all over to me. You don't even need to figure out a solution. Give Me the problems and I'll in return gives you all of the solutions. I AM. Let Me be I AM to you. All you have to do is trust Me. I know everything there is to know about you.

Surrender your all to Me now. That's the only thing I ask of you. Don't even focus on the past and the things you've been through. Look ahead and only focus on the future. You and I have so much work to do.

TRUST

NEVER ALONE

The Father never leaves us alone. Whatever we may go through He's right there. Sometimes it may seem as if you have no help, but just because it 'seems', doesn't mean that's the way it is. All we have to do is reach up with our faith and trust and depend totally on Him. We are only here for a short while. He is here to help us along the way. Even when we may be in a very tough spot, we must always remember what our Father promised us. He cannot lie. He said he would never leave us or forsake of. When we praise Him, we cause Him to move for us faster than ever before. He is always on our side and for us. His hands are always extended towards us. Now reach up and grabbed His hand and let Him take you through, around, or over the situation. Most important let Him fight the battle and you just breathe and relax in his arms.

THE RING OF LIFE

There are three classes in the ring of life. First there's lightweight. In this class you have help and people around to guide you as you approach the blows. They are there to help you to mature your skills, to give you the basics that you would never forget. This class is a symbol of your childhood.

The next class is middleweight. This class is a step above lightweight. The people that once surrounded you began to drift away. You are learning independence. You are adherent to your heart and to the voice of God as he speaks to you. As you face the obstacles that come you are learning to deal with them and to bounce back. This class is also a symbol of your young child.

Finally, you have advanced to heavyweight. You have reached the most advanced levels all. This class says, 'I'm ready for life.' You are taking the blows of life, but they don't faze you the way they did at the middleweight level.

All your skills and basic training from your two previous levels are blossoming. They have reached their full peak. You are now equipped for life. Whatever life throws your way you are equipped to deal with it and overcome. You are learning the abilities and skills that are inside of you that you thought did not exist. You are now ready to help others. It is not you that it is Christ that lives within you and empowering you to go forth.

FIRST LOVE

Just about everyone has a first love. The humanly first love is somewhat selfish. Sometimes it can have limits on it. The first love between a man and a woman say; 'my love only goes so far. If you do this or that I'm gone.'

God's love always says come back to me no matter what you have done. When a person experiences the love of God for the first time they are overwhelmed. God is their first love. He is all they ever hoped for. He is everything they could have ever dreamed or imagined. His love comes into their hearts and fills every void that they may have. It doesn't come inside of them alone. It comes with peace and such joy; a joy that can't be explained by the greatest poet of all times. It makes you feel like no one could feel this happy and still be living. We must never leave God for He is our first love. He beckons unto us to come back home. No loves can ever compare to His. It is so powerful, yet not controlling.

Because you back
each time for more.
Stay with the first
love of all loves; God.

INNER MAN

We were all born with the inner man. Everyone may not have been born rich, poor, black, white, that for small. But every one of us was born with the inner man. He talks to us. Each one of us raises our inner man and matures him by what we feed him. When we go to the grocery store, we want to feed our bodies. We also go to the store (that is, the church) to feed our inner man words of life. He lives and grows also about words. We are held accountable for the words to see him.

Don't ever see him words of death; it will only destroy him because these words grow inside of him. They don't produce anything good but instead they will produce everything evil. We must (meaning there are no ifs, ands, or buts about it). Feed him words of life. we feed him these words by what we speak from our mouths. So be careful what you say. Your words are responsible for the kind of inner man that will grow up inside of you. Let him be full of **LIFE**.

PLEASING

From the time we are children we strive to please someone. Then, we look for their words of encouragement as we strive to please them. There should be a point in our lives that this end. You see, pleasing people is something you never really can do. No matter what you do, with some people it would never be enough. What about the phrase;' I wonder what he/she will say?' There you go still trying to please people. In order to experience true happiness, you must stop trying to please people. In this life is something you want to do makes you happy and God is pleased with what you want to do I say go for it. Don't tell too many people about it either. Just do it, and then they will see. When you are a God pleaser and not a people pleaser, then you know that you are free. We must strive to please Him more than anyone else. You cannot please everyone, but you can please the **One, and the ONLY GOD!!!** If it is all right with

God then you know you are on course. You please God and let Him deal with the people, and then you are *pleasing.*

IT'S ALL ABOUT GOD

Everything I do is because of Him. There's nothing that I do alone. So, for me, *it's all about God.*

As I open my eyes each morning, I give thanks to Him. He has blessed me with such a wonderful husband so I give Him praise. I thank Him for my prosperous children and their lives. *It's all about God.*

His love for me never ends. Look at how awesome He is. Just to behold His hands or any part of Him would be such a precious and joyous moment. *It's all about God.*

If I never please anyone down here it will be all right. So, I will and I must strive to please Him. His name has more meaning than any name on this earth. People write love songs to one another. The number one love song is the one about

God; IT'S **ALL ABOUT GOD.**

He is unlimited, powerful, merciful, the many breasted One, Almighty, Sustainer, and My Provider. There is no end of to His name. Wherever I go and whatever I do each day I'm on this earth I will let him walk me through it. For me: **IT'S ALL ABOUT GOD.**

THE WORD

The word is the only truth we have to hold on to today. It is the only true book of our times. It is the most powerful tool that anyone can use. You can go to it and find an everyday solution for whatever the problem may be. There is no problem in this life that only applies to a certain group of people. Anyone can give their life to Christ and then begin to partake in this great everyday living. I believe we all need to define help of the Master and all of heaven. Take the Word and have faith to believe and apply it. For the Word is the only truth we have today.

THIS DAY

Help me, Father to accomplish whatever task I may face this day.

I look to you to be my guide.

I won't look at the things behind.

I will strive for the things ahead.

I know that each day is a step towards my final accomplishment.

Every step I take I will let you decide.

I will never face life alone.

There's nothing I would do without putting you first.

You are my first love.

PASSING THROUGH

We all are just passing through in this life. Life is the past that leads to eternity. The past our final destination is all up to us on an individual basis. No one can determine the path for a another. There are only two paths to

choose from. The
choices are life
eternal or eternal
damnation. No one
can really know in
their hearts when the
path of life would
take them to their
final destination. One
thing we can be sure
of is the path that will
open up to us. We

know this by the way that we live as we passed through. It can be compared to a tunnel. As we walked through the tunnel of life we must fulfill our destination. When we come to the end of the tunnel, we may see light or darkness but it's all up to us.

LIFE'S JOURNEY

I am traveling down life's journey.

It's a journey that awaits me with so many quests.

Each day I awake and wonder of what quests I will be on.

Someday I may be on a quest that I don't really understand why I'm on it.

As the days go on and a new quest unfolds, I understand the quests that I did not understand before.

Sometimes a quest may lead me to multiple roads, and there I must choose the most successful road of all. There are even times, when I'm somewhere that no one can understand me at all.

It is then I depend on my God to walk me down the road to hold and comfort my soul.

To have Him with me on each quest is a blessing.

I can never travel this journey without Him.

Each day He walked me through a new quest. He teaches me something new at every beginning.

Made in the USA
Monee, IL
22 January 2022

88895764R00115